The Birmingham Greenway

by
Fred Willits

MERIDIAN BOOKS

Published 2000 by Meridian Books
© Frederick Willits 2000

ISBN 1-869922-40-9
A catalogue record for this book is available from
the British Library.

Meridian Books
40 Hadzor Road, Oldbury, West Midlands B68 9LA
Printed in Great Britain by MFP Design & Print, Manchester.

Contents

Publishers' Note

Every care has been taken in the preparation of this book. All sections of the walk have been independently checked and are believed to be correct at the time of publication. However, no guarantee can be given that they contain no errors or omissions and neither the author nor the publishers can accept any responsibility for loss, damage or inconvenience resulting from the use of this book.

Birmingham does not publish a definitive map and it is therefore not possible to confirm that any path is a right of way. However, all the paths in this book are well walked and there is no reason to believe that there should be any problems of access. However, in the unlikely event of your encountering any difficulties the publishers would be very pleased to have details.

Using this book

ALTHOUGH the total length of this walk is 23 miles the ready availability of public transport means that you can choose to do the walk in one go or in shorter sections as time or inclination permits. The locations of suitable bus stops and railway stations are indicated in the text, and it is suggested that you have with you a Birmingham bus map that can be obtained from Centro and Travel West Midlands travel centres, where you can also collect relevant timetables. In Birmingham city centre the Centro travel centre is in the forecourt to New Street station; the TWM travel centre is in The Pavilions (lower ground floor).

The sketch maps incorporated in the text are intended as a guide but you will probably like to have with you a Birmingham A to Z Street Atlas in case weather or other reason makes you wish to vary your route.

Much of the walk is on grass and footpaths although some tarmac is inevitable. All of the walking is easy and should not present any difficulties. However, some of the paths in Sutton Park can be muddy after rain, so stout footwear, especially in wet periods, is recommended here.

Acknowledgements

I AM indebted to the many members of City of Birmingham Ramblers who encouraged me to consider publishing this walk and who subsequently walked the paths to ensure that the directions were accurate. I would especially like to thank Edna Irwin and Peter Groves for their invaluable help in providing much of the additional material that accompanies the walking instructions, and to Edna also for word processing the text.

My thanks likewise to Steve Brittain, Bill Dewar, Nigel Groves, Pat Holmes, Tony Holmes, Joan Jenkinson, the Chamberlain Park Hotel and to the staff of the Local Studies Department of Birmingham City Library, all of whom provided me with additional material and/or photographs.

Fred Willits

Introduction

THIS walk, which extends from the present north-east boundary of Birmingham to the south-west boundary, was first devised in 1990 to celebrate the tenth anniversary of the founding of the City of Birmingham Group of the Ramblers' Association. Then, in 1995, this being the diamond jubilee year of the Ramblers' Association as well as the fifteenth anniversary of the City of Birmingham Group, members of the public were invited to join the Group in another walking of the route on Saturday 22nd July.

Although the complete walk is 23 miles in length it can be divided up into shorter lengths as it was in July 1995. The walk crosses the many open spaces still accessible to the public within the city boundary and yet is convenient to public transport. In addition it gives an insight into the social and industrial development of the city and gives a glimpse of attempts to integrate members of the multi-ethnic community of Birmingham today.

Members of the Birmingham Group of the Ramblers' Association at the start of their walk along the Birmingham Greenway in 1995

About the Author

FRED WILLITS was born in 1933, the youngest of three children. He lived in Tower Road, Aston until the age of three when, as he says, "the family moved upmarket into a house with both a front *and* a back door". He attended Vicarage Road Infant and Junior Schools until being evacuated to Ravenstone, Leicestershire when the war started in 1939. On his return to Birmingham he went to Upper Thomas Street Senior School (next to the HP Sauce factory) and hoped then to be able to study at the Birmingham School of Art. However, this was not to be and he joined the R.A.F. for three years, then went to a technical college to learn carpentry, a trade that he applied working for a firm making hospital furniture.

He has been an enthusiastic walker since 1968. He was Ramblers' Association Footpath Secretary for the West Midlands County until 1984 when the City of Birmingham Group of the RA was formed of which Fred was a founder member. He then became Footpath Secretary of this group, a position that he still holds. He is an active member of the Group's Footpath Maintenance Team which cooperates with the Warwickshire local authority in erecting waymark posts, stiles and footbridges. He has served on the Midlands Area Council of the Ramblers' Association and has been a delegate to the National Council several times.

He led his first walk in 1970 and now, as well as periodically leading for the Birmingham Group, often acts as a back marker, being instantly recognisable by his coloured woolly hat. His schoolboy passion for train spotting and cigarette cards was extended to collecting the numbers of Ordnance Survey trig points, sometimes resulting in his veering away from a main group of walkers to study a nearby point. He is an enthusiastic chess player and is a member of the Birmingham Chess League.

Fred has an encyclopaedic knowledge of paths and walkways in Birmingham and is currently engaged in a project to transfer all the information that he has on these into computer readable form, an especially valuable activity since Birmingham does not yet have a definitive map.

1

Watford Gap to Sutton Park – Banners Gate

5 miles

START: On the A4026 to the east of Blake Street station and Watford Gap at the junction of Watford Gap Road with Hillwood Common Road and Little Hay Lane – A-Z page 27 3H.
PUBLIC TRANSPORT: Rail: Birmingham Cross City line to Blake Street Station. On leaving the station turn right (east) along the A4026 (Blake Street). At the crossroads cross the A4512 and continue forward along Watford Gap Road to reach the starting point at the next crossroads.
Buses: TWM Service 102 Birmingham City Centre/Hill Hook. Alight at the junction with the A4026 (Blake Street/Watford Gap Road) and walk along Watford Gap Road to reach the starting point at the next crossroads.

WALKING west along Watford Gap Road, heading towards Blake Street station, the walk commences in a relatively rural setting; to the left is the BBC television mast and on a clear day, to the right, there are views to Lichfield and Cannock Chase. At the first crossroads what was once an old farmhouse (Watford House) is now a nursing home – a sign of the times. At this crossroads turn left into Lichfield Road (A5127); here one crosses the City boundary and is greeted by the sign 'Royal Town of Sutton Coldfield' a reminder

The starting point of the walk

9

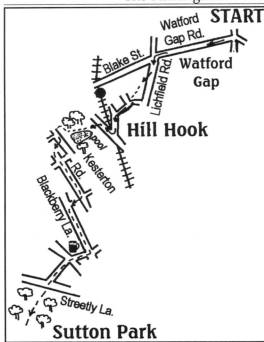

that, until 1974, Sutton Coldfield was a borough in its own right.

Cross to the right-hand side of the road and a garden centre (Windley). At the boundary fence of the garden centre turn right and walk diagonally across the open space to reach the junction of Vaughan Close and Bishops Way. Cross over Vaughan Close, turn right and walk along Bishops Way, crossing to the left side of the road.

102 bus route near the shops.

At the roundabout take the left exit (still Bishops Way) and continue to a T-junction. Here turn right to enter Hill Hook Road (and rejoin the 102 bus route and 112 bus route from the City Centre to Lichfield; note the change of architecture).

Cross to the left-hand side of the road and after crossing the railway line take the first turn on the left into Netherstone Grove. At the T-junction cross over to a

The Sutton Coldfield Television Mast

The land on which the mast is erected was common land until the Enclosure Act of 1835. The site is 570 ft above sea level. Work started on the first mast in 1949 and was completed in 1950. It was the first mast outside London, and at that time was the world's most powerful with a radius of 50 miles and weighing 140 tons. It had a lift and, to prevent it icing, a heater.

On the day that it opened 13,000 people turned up resulting in Sutton Coldfield's worst traffic jam!

footpath directly opposite. This leads to Hill Hook Nature Reserve. Before crossing the bridge, the site of an old corn mill can be seen on the right.

Follow the path along the side of the reservoir, enjoying the water birds; leave the reserve at Bradgate Drive on the right. Bear right, and follow the drive to house number 23. Just past it turn left into the cul-de-sac and cross it to enter a cycle/walk way at the top to reach Clarence Road.

112 bus route City Centre/Lichfield.

Turn left, cross the road and continue to house number 349. Here take the path on the right and continue up an incline to Kesterton Road. Turn left and walk to a crossroads.

Go straight over to walk along White Farm Road. At house number 19 take the footpath on the right; follow it to Blackberry Lane (no blackberries now!) and continue left to a T-junction. Here turn right up Four Oaks Common Road. At the next crossroads – The Crown pub is on the corner – continue straight ahead to cross over the A454 (Walsall

Bus service 966 .

> **Birmingham City Boundaries**
>
> With population changes and re-developments there have been a number of changes to the boundaries of the city of Birmingham, mainly linked with expansion. A major change occurred in 1974 when the Royal Burgh of Sutton Coldfield came within the city boundary, despite opposition of its residents. The walk crosses the former boundary line.

> **Hill Hook Corn Mill.**
>
> The mill is known to have been in existence in 1691 and was operating until 1914, although it was not vacated until 1968. In the intervening years it was used as a café for a period and in the 1920s was popular for Sunday school outings. Linked with vandalism it was demol- ished in 1970. In January 1987 the land and pool became a Nature Reserve.
>
> In its heyday the mill had sole access to a water supply covering three acres. The mill wheel, measuring 12 ft in diameter and 6 ft in width is preserved at Forge Mill in Sandwell.

Hill Hook Nature Reserve

Road) and enter Crown Lane. Follow Crown Lane to its junction with Streetly Lane.

Here turn right and immediately cross to the other side of the road and enter Sutton Park.

Sutton Park contains a maze of paths. Follow the instructions carefully to avoid going off-route.

On entering the park cross the perimeter path and take the middle of the three paths facing you. After a short way through a wooded area the path continues to more open space, where silver birches have been removed to encourage the development of heathland.

Cross a track here and continue forward, soon crossing another track. Ignore a minor path going diag-

The Crown

onally left. *Note the many holly trees in this area.* Cross a third track when the path soon veers to the right and descends to Bracebridge Pool.

Just before reaching the edge of the pool take the path on the left that runs parallel with the edge of the pool, crossing a number of footbridges. (*The number is a closely guarded secret as it is said that parents use them for counting practice for their young off-*

The start of the walk through Sutton Park

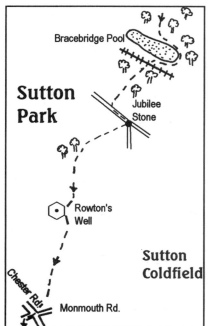

spring!) The path emerges from the woods at The Boathouse restaurant.

Turn right towards the pool, then turn left and continue walking beside it in front of the restaurant. Follow the main path beyond the pool and cross the railway bridge on the left. Follow the main path diagonally right; this swings left and after about 150 yards reaches a Y-junction of paths. Here take the right fork to emerge from the woods at an 'ungated' gatepost. Take a path diagonally left from the gate, and follow it to a

Sutton Park

Sutton Park has recently been added to the English Heritage register of parks and gardens. It is of considerable archaeological interest – evidence of an ancient encampment and a Roman road.

Although development of the area dates back at least to Roman times and there is evidence of an ancient encampment and a Roman road – the Roman road Ryknield remains as a public highway – the area which is known to-day as Sutton only became known by this name in the reign of King Athelstan (AD925-940), when it received its first Royal Charter. It became an important hunting area – 'Chase' – and was extensively hunted by the kings of Mercia until it came into the possession of the Crown after the Norman Conquest. Subsequently the forest, in a deal with Henry I in 1129, came into the possession of the Earls of Warwick, who were often absentee landlords.

Later the Chase reverted to the Crown until, under the influence of Bishop Vesey, Henry VIII, in 1528, granted a royal charter to Sutton Coldfield, which also granted Sutton Woods to the inhabitants of the Royal Burgh in perpetuity.

Sutton Park has an area of 2400 acres of which approximately twenty per cent is woodland. The circumference is in the region of seven miles; there are seven pools – man-made – extending over 70 acres. Three of the pools date back to medieval times, the others being developed in relation to the thirteen water mills which operated at one time.

On the fourth of August 1868 there was a 'Great Fire' when somewhere between 300 and 1000 acres were alight. In the twentieth century the Park had an important role as a military training ground and was also a popular venue for sport and entertainment.

Bracebridge Pool

This, one of the three medieval pools, is named after Sir Ralph Bracebridge who leased the Manor and Chase of Sutton Coldfield from the Earls of Warwick early in the fifteenth century. He built the pool to ensure a supply of bream for his own use, in addition to those that he had to supply as rent! The pool covers an area of 35 acres.

The Scout Jamboree Memorial Stone

tarmac road. Turn left and walk for about 200 yards (passing road gates) to a fork in the road.

In the island between the roads is the Jamboree Memorial Stone, commemorating the Scout Jamboree held in the park in August 1957.

Take the right-hand road and at the jamboree stone turn right

Bracebridge Pool

JAMBOREE SITE FLOODED IN NIGHT STORM

Thousands of Scouts Leave Tents

SHELTER APPEAL IN EMERGENCY

THOUSANDS of Scouts at the Jamboree had to leave their tents at Sutton Park early to-day when one of the worst thunderstorms in the Midlands for many years flooded the camping sites.

How the Birmingham Post reported the 1957 flood in Sutton Park

again along a gravel track, in a westerly direction, towards woodland. Reaching an area of gorse and heather the view opens up and Barr Beacon can be seen in the distance on the right. (*A high point with a memorial to men and women of Staffordshire killed in the First World War.*) On reaching a pine wood on the right there are two paths on the left at right angles to the main track, the first just as you reach the trees, the second just a few yards further on and opposite a large holly bush. Take the second of these paths, going through a short grassy area and then descending towards Rowton's Well – an ancient source of water. You will soon reach a crossroads of paths – here continue straight forward along a grassy path. *Don't be tempted away to the left by a more clearly defined path.* After about 75 yards the path swings

---

The Jamboree Memorial Stone

Sutton Park was the venue for a world jamboree held in August 1957 to commemorate fifty years of scouting and the centenary of Lord Baden-Powell the founder of the movement. (The Girl Guides had their own international camp at the same time in Windsor Great Park.) The weather had been exceptionally dry before the opening of the camp and during the first few days, so that when the there was a torrential downpour – shortly after the visit of the Queen and Prince Philip – the water was not readily absorbed and flooded through some of the site.

The 'flood' was exaggerated by the press and the Guides were not too displeased to learn of the discomfort of the scouts! Local residents are remembered for the assistance they gave in drying out sodden clothes and bedding. The event is commemorated by the 'Jamboree' stone.

Rowton's Well

right to reach the well *which is not visible until you are close to it.*

Past the well continue along the path (with the well on the right), ignoring a path almost immediately off to the left, to reach a good footbridge on the right over a stream – it can be extremely muddy around here at certain times. Note Longmoor Pool some distance to the left, as you

Rowton's Well
This has always been an important source of water and it is alleged that from time immemorial the water was believed to have healing properties, especially for eye diseases.

follow the path to the car park at Banners Gate. Turn right to leave the park at Banners Gate. (Junction of Monmouth Drive and Chester Road North A452).

Bus service 113/113X City Centre/Streetly stops in Chester Road North. Service 377 Sutton Coldfield/Streetly stops in Banners Gate Road.

2

Banner's Gate to Aston Hall

5 miles

A T Banners Gate turn right to cross Chester Road North at the traffic lights and walk along the left-hand side of Banners Gate Road opposite. At the corner of The Greenway and Banners Gate Road enter the recreation area and walk diagonally up to the crest of the hill and the former City of Birmingham boundary. Continue along the same line, walking between houses on the left and a fence on the right to reach Banners Walk and then King's Road.

At the T-junction, cross the road (pedestrian crossing on the right) and enter Kingstanding Recreation Ground facing. Do not follow the tarmac path but walk diagonally down to the corner of the fence on the left and follow it with the brook on the right to Homerton Road. Cross over the road and continue across the recreation ground, parallel with the brook (now culverted), to College

The brook at Marsh Hill

18

Road (dual carriageway)

 Bus services 107 Birmingham/ Sutton Coldfield and 113 Birmingham/Streetly.

Cross College Road, and enter Hurstwood Road/ Maxted Road directly opposite. At the Hurstway on the left, walk up the grassy slope, facing and walk above and parallel to Hurstwood Road and then Maxted Road. Cross The Hurstway and continue on grass to the T-junction with Witton Lodge Road. *If you look left here you will get a good view of Oscott College.*

 Bus service 7 Birmingham/Perry Common.

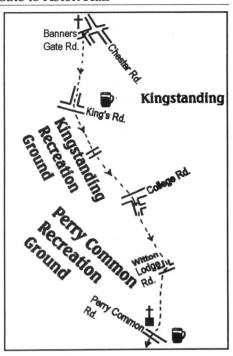

Witton Lakes

Brookvale and Witton Lakes

When a waterworks company was formed in 1826 the lakes were acquired and later dammed to increase the water supply. In 1856 the Waterworks company bought 32 acres of land from a Mr Wyrley Birch for £3,600. In 1909 Erdington council (still outside the Birmingham boundary) acquired the waterworks and the area was opened as a park. What had been known as Lower Witton Reservoir became Brookvale Park and the upper and middle reservoirs as Witton Park

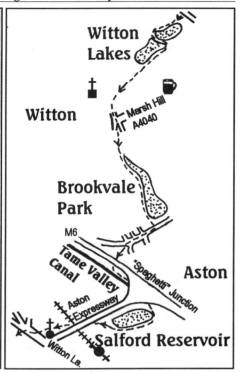

Cross Witton Lodge Road at the crossing, turn right and then go left into Perry Common Recreation Ground just before the boundary fence/hedge. Cross the open space, heading for the left-hand corner of a metal fence ahead, to reach St Margaret and St Mary Junior and Infant School. Skirt the school and arrive at Perry Common Road.

Bus service 28, and a pub (O'Shea's) to the left).

Cross the road and go across the grass, veering slightly to the right to reach Witton Lakes.

On the right note the large educational campus – the site of special schools for the visually impaired, hearing impaired and physically handicapped.

Walk beside the first lake (on your left), then cross the causeway dividing the lakes. At the end of the causeway turn right on to a grass track and follow the path up the incline – to get a better view. At the hedge turn right and continue beside it beyond the lake and its dam, ignoring the turning off to a bridge over the dam. Pass an electricity transformer and walk beside a brook on your right to reach a metal fence and Marsh Hill, at Marsh Hill Junior and Infant school.

11 Outer Circle bus route.

On the left is the Mill House pub.

Cross Marsh Hill (A4040) and turn right. Immediately on the left enter Boulton Walk. At the first intersection walk diagonally across an open space to cross George Road and enter Brookvale Park.

Turn left along a tarmac path, then veer left to walk beside a

---

Oscott College

The college (St. Mary's) which opened in the 1830s, is now the seminary of Birmingham Archdiocese and the main training college for its priests in the Roman Catholic church. Clerical students also come from other dioceses in England and Wales.

The site is said to have been chosen for its remoteness at that time. The present college replaced an earlier educational church establishment and was the brainchild of Bishop Thomas Walsh who was the president of the original college which catered for lay and clerical students.

The original architect was Joseph Potter of Lichfield and an important benefactor was the Earl of Shrewsbury. He had been employing the architect and decorator Augustus Pugin at Alton Towers and introduced him to Bishop Walsh with the re-sult that Pugin replaced Joseph Potter when the college was nearing completion. Pugin became responsible for much of the internal decoration, especially of the chapel.

The college functioned as an educational establishment for lay and clerical students until 1891 when it relinquished its role in educating laity, and the clerical students from Olton seminary moved across to Oscott.

Many well-known converts to Catholicism were attracted to Oscott; one of these was an ancestor of the late Diana, Princess of Wales. He was the Honourable and Reverend George Spencer, the convert son of Viscount Althorp: in the 1840s he was spiritual director at the college. Another convert with connections with Oscott was John Henry Newman who was confirmed as a Catholic in the chapel at Oscott.

Birmingham Canals

Much of Birmingham's prosperity is based on the canals which in the late seventeenth and the eighteenth centuries provided a highly efficient means of transport for fuel, raw materials and finished goods for the town's rapidly growing industries.

The first of Birmingham's canals was built by James Brindley and provided a link to the Staffordshire & Worcestershire Canal at Aldersley Junction, north of Wolverhampton. The first section was opened in 1769 and connected Birmingham with the collieries at Wednesbury, leading to a dramatic drop in the price of coal. The value of shares in the company, initially issued at £140 each, had exceeded £1,000 some twenty-five years later.

This was soon followed by the Birmingham & Fazeley Canal, built by James Smeaton and completed in 1790. The companies owning the two canals amalgamated and in 1794 adopted the name of the Birmingham Canal Navigations. In the following years many more canals were built and incorporated into the network and in 1895 the company owned about 160 miles of canal, just over 100 miles of which remain today.

The Tame Valley Canal, part of which is followed in Chapter 2, was built much later in 1844, well into the railway age. By then canal building techniques had greatly developed and whereas the earlier canals meandered around, keeping as far as possible to a constant contour, the Tame Valley Canal goes through deep cuttings and along high embankments.

The Grand Union Canal links Birmingham to London and is an amalgamation of eight separate canals. It includes the Birmingham and Warwick Junction Canal, the building of which was completed in 1844 and provided a by-pass to the Birmingham & Fazeley, passage along which was very slow due to numerous locks. Much of the Grand Union was modernised in the 1930s in what proved to be a vain attempt to beat off competition from rail and road transport. This involved the widening of the original narrow locks to take 70 ton barges, and the construction of branches to many important towns. However, this was not done for the section walked in Chapter 3 where the old narrow locks, which will only take boats of up to 7 ft width, remain.

brook on the left; continue beside a lake to Brookvale Sailing Club on the right and reaching Park Road. (Note the car park and the site for disabled fishers). From the boat-house turn right into Park Road and go up North Park Road, crossing to the left-hand side. Note the ornithological character of the road names.

When you reach Stonechat Drive on the left cross this and immediately turn left at a paved footpath (with lamps); follow this up to its highest point, where there are views of Aston Expressway and Aston Park. Continue down on the path to cross under the M6 (Aston Villa football club building can be seen ahead), staying on the right-hand side until the Tame Valley Canal is reached. Now in the midst of a pocket of Birmingham industry turn right down to the towpath and then make a U-turn to pass under the bridge and follow the towpath to Witton Turnover Bridge.

Turn right to cross the bridge. Turn left and walk along the towpath passing under a National Grid service bridge, a railway bridge, a maze of motorways ('Spaghetti Junction') and through

---

'Spaghetti Junction' (Gravelly Hill Interchange)

Situated at Aston, the interchange was built between 1968 and 1971 by Sir Owen Williams and Partners to provide an exit from the M6 and access to North and Central Birmingham. It is above the formerly named Aston Reservoir, now known as Salford Park, which belonged to Aston Manor Waterworks. (Salford bridge was opened in 1924). The area was known as a busy site for transport communication with trams and buses, and Aston station (Cross City line) is nearby. The first electric tram to pass through the area was in 1907 from the City Centre to Chester Road. This was preceded by steam trams and double-decker buses (1885). In 1922 Lichfield Road – from Salford Bridge to King Edward's pub – was widened so that trams could run down the centre of the road.

Aston Expressway was designed and built by the City engineers and was opened in 1972; it carries a 'vinegar' drain (*see box on page 31*). From it there is a good view of Aston Hall, Aston church and modern developments on the former Holte estate. The tower blocks (built in the 1950s) bear the names of former eminent Birmingham men e.g. Boulton, Watt, Murdoch and Priestley.

a dark, wide tunnel to emerge into daylight. Just before the next road bridge (Salford Bridge, with a 'Welcome to Heartlands' plaque) and at the site of the former toll house guarding the junction with the Birmingham & Fazeley Canal, turn right and ascend a tarmac slope to gain the A5127 Lichfield Road.

Bus route 104 and many other buses to and from the City Centre; Aston station on the Cross-city line is also nearby).

To view the confluence of the Hockley Brook and the Tame continue

Aston Villa Football Club

The club dates from 1874 when members of the local Wesleyan Chapel Sunday School formed a football team. Games were originally played in Aston Park, moving to Wellington Road, Perry Barr in 1876.

In 1888 Aston Villa were founder members of the Football League, a competition for which William McGregor, a Villa committee member, had been a driving force.

In 1896, the club took out a twenty-one year lease on Aston Lower Grounds (part of the original Aston Hall estate) at a rent of £300 per annum with an option to buy at £10,000. It was officially opened on 17 April 1897 when Villa played Blackburn Rovers with an attendance of 15,000. The ground was developed over the next fourteen years to accommodate 70,000 spectators. It became Villa Park in 1898 and the land was purchased in 1911. Today's pitch is on the site of an ancient fishpond. There was a walled kitchen garden on the site of the present North Stand and nearby was the Staffordshire Pool, used as a boating lake and as a skating rink in winter.

Three of the four current stands have been built since 1977. The Trinity Road stand was originally built in 1923 although there are plans to develop this in order to increase capacity from 40,000 to 50,000.

Villa Park is considered one of the premier stadiums in the country and was used as a venue for some of the games in the World Cup in 1966, for the European Championships in 1996, and for the European Cup Winners Cup Final in May 1999.

On the playing front, Aston Villa have been one of the country's most successful teams having won both the League Championship and the FA Cup on seven occasions each. Their greatest achievement was to win the European Cup in 1982. The League Cup, which they won in 1895, was stolen from a shop window where it was on display, and was never recovered.

along the towpath and up a concrete ramp under the A5127 to the bridge over the Birmingham & Fazeley canal. Below the canal the Tame is the river emerging from the culvert on the right, the Hockley Brook joining it from the left, parallel with, but below the level of the canal. Return to the A5127.

Turn right and cross the bridge over the River Tame. Immediately after crossing the bridge turn right onto a tarmac path to enter Salford Park. The path continues below Spaghetti Junction (Graveley Hill Interchange) with the Tame, which had to be diverted to facilitate the building of Spaghetti Junction, on the right.

Brookvale Park

You soon reach Salford Reservoir, which used to belong to Aston Manor Waterworks. *Here you have a choice of routes.* You can either turn left to walk along the left side of the reservoir or continue forward along the right-hand side. The right-hand route is shorter but going along the left side gives a rather better view of the reservoir and keeps you further away from the motorway.

Reaching the end of the reservoir turn right and walk towards the motorway. Cross a bridge over the River Tame, noticing in microcosm the history of the development of transport – the canal, the railway and the motorway following the same path, presumably the line of least resistance. Immediately after crossing the river turn left along a tarmac path, between columns, below the road, towards and under a railway bridge. Reaching Electric Avenue turn left under the Aston Expressway – A38(M). Cross the road and turn right into Aston Hall Road.

Aston Church

The origins of the church, dedicated to St Peter, go back to Saxon times but in the mid-nineteenth century there was a major reconstruction. Many interesting effigies are preserved in the church and in the graveyard are tombs of the Ansell family.

At the corner note the staircase on the left, ascending to the railway line close to where the Birmingham Cross City and the Birmingham-Walsall–Hednesford lines diverge.

Walk along Aston Hall Road, passing the Aston Villa sports and leisure centre on the right. Note the remains of a colourful mural at the end of the car park. On the opposite side of the road an industrial development occupies the site of former almshouses. On the right, immediately after passing under the Expressway, is an old building currently boarded up (and perhaps due for demolition) – *a plaque on the wall just above ground*

The Ansell family graves in Aston church

level and to the right of the first door commemorates this as the site of 'Ye Old Aston Tavern', built in 1561.

After crossing the road on the right take the path on the immediate right into the churchyard of Aston Old Church. Following the path to the right of the church pass the graves of the Ansell (brewery) family, and a Garden of Remembrance on the left in a corner adjacent to a recent extension to the church. Due to the risk of vandalism the church is unlikely to be open for the casual visitor. Circle the extension to regain the main path and emerge on Witton Lane opposite the entrance to Aston Hall.

 Bus services 440 (Birmingham/Bearwood/Perry Barr) and 40X (Limited service Bearwood/Handsworth/Witton).

Aston Onion Fair

This was a six day event, originally held in the Bull Ring area, dating from medieval times and celebrating the arrival of the first onions of the season. However, it was more than an agricultural event and was accompanied by funfairs and other forms of entertainment. It was not to the liking of many residents and in 1781 was described as 'the lowest of low amusements: riot, drunkenness and mischief'. Entertainment was abolished in 1875 and the fair then moved beyond the control of the Birmingham authorities to the Old Pleck at Aston – a site in the bow of the river Tame behind Aston church. It remained here, as Pat Collins' Fair, until 1969 when the Aston Expressway was cut through the site.

3

Aston Hall to Camp Hill

4 miles

FROM Witton Lane enter the grounds of Aston Hall. Turn left and after passing a row of trees turn right and walk up the grass between an 'avenue' of trees to the main entrance of Aston Hall, just below the clock tower. (The approach to the hall can be made by the tarmac drive but the view is less dramatic!)

Note the old Birmingham coat of arms on the right and the Squirrel of the Ansell family on the left as you approach the steps.

At the top of the steps continue forward to a flower-bed; turn right through an archway and then immediately left to circle the Hall counter clockwise.

At the T-junction Villa supporters might like to make a diversion to the right, though the view of the Villa stands is somewhat obscured in the summer by trees. Having gazed your fill turn round and walk back to the hall and continue with the building on the left.

At the end of the Hall turn left at the (modern railed) arcade. At the T-junction turn right and at the end of the car park turn left and immediately right to walk along the main drive, which then becomes Upper Thomas Street.

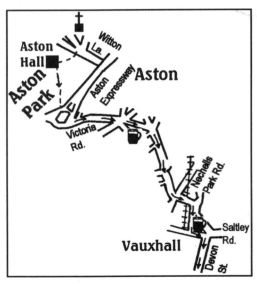

On the right is King Edward VI Grammar School for Boys. You might like to climb up the grassy slope opposite the school to obtain a view of the City Centre and the BT Tower. You may, if the wind is in the right direction, detect an appetising aroma from the HP Sauce factory which you can also see.

Continue along Upper Thomas Street, crossing the end of Albert Road, to enter the subway opposite. Cross under an approach road to the Aston Expressway; turn left immediately on emerging in the centre of the roundabout; walk up the incline, cross over the Aston Expressway (to be greeted by a 1993 sculp-

Aston Hall and Park

Aston Hall, built by Sir Thomas Holte, Lord of the Manor of Aston and first baronet, between 1618 and 1635, is late Jacobean in style. The Holtes remained at Aston, despite major financial problems until 1817 when the estate was dispersed to pay off creditors and the contents sold.

The Hall was then leased out to James Watt junior, the son of the famous engineer. Following his death in 1848 it was hoped to acquire the Hall and park for the town of Birmingham. There was prolonged haggling over the price and it was only in 1856 that Birmingham withdrew and a committee was formed to raise funds for the purchase of Aston Hall.

This became the Aston Hall and Park Company and although only ten per cent of the purchase price had been paid this new centre of entertainment was opened to the public by Queen Victoria in 1858. In the grounds of the Hall there was music, skating (when the lake was frozen over), circuses and many other entertainments and sporting events. In 1879 one of the first football matches to be floodlit, between Birmingham and Nottingham, was held there. The site is now occupied by the Aston Villa ground.

At a fete in 1863, a female tightrope walker was killed in an unfortunate accident. The Queen was indignant, particularly when she learnt that the Hall and park were still not paid for. Further funds were raised by public subscription and the remainder of the debt was paid by Birmingham Council and the Hall was taken over by the City of Birmingham. It is managed by Birmingham Leisure Services and deserves to be better known.

In October 1642 the Holtes gave shelter overnight to King Charles I before the battle of Edgehill and in December the house was attacked by Parliamentarians over a three day period. Damage to the great staircase can still be seen.

ture, 'Face to Face'). Swing left to go under Park Circus round-about. Ahead with a gas holder in view is Victoria Road and parallel on the right, the newly developed Waterlinks Boulevard. This is now Heartlands. Walk left down Victoria Road.

Aston Hall

King Edward VI Grammar School, Aston

Following a petition from the inhabitants, the first free grammar school in Birmingham was established by letters patent of King Edward VI that were sealed on 2nd January 1552. The school was located in New Street and remained there for four centuries

In the eighteenth century the Governors of the King Edward VI Foundation 'being truly sensible that great numbers of children in this place by reason of the poverty or the negligence of their parents, are never taught to read the English tongue'

moved to establish further schools and to provide education for girls. In 1752 two masters and two mistresses were appointed at £15 a year. Other schools were subsequently established with six being opened in 1883, one being the Aston school with accommodation for both boys and girls, the girls being moved to Handsworth in 1911. It has remained on its present site since then but was extensively modernised in 1962 and additional facilities were added in 1986.

Bus services 440 (Birmingham/Bearwood/Perry Barr) and 40X (Limited service Bearwood/Handsworth/Witton).

When Victoria Road swings off to the left turn right to the pedestrian crossing and cross over the dual carriageway (Lichhfield Road).

Several bus services to Birmingham and Sutton Coldfield.

Turn left to pass the Vine public house and then turn right into Sandy Lane. Follow the pavement down and cross the road to

---

HP Sauce

The recipe for 'Houses of Parliament Sauce' was bought from Garton's grocers in Nottingham by Edwin Sampson Moore. In 1875 he established a factory in Tower Road in Aston on account of the excellent quality of the well water available. The sauce is now sold in 113 countries.

The factory is on a split site and the sauce and vinegar factories are joined by a pipeline, the so-called 'vinegar drain'.

The tower with the HP logo was not built until 1975 and in 1986 the tower and factory were modernised. At the time that the Aston Expressway was being planned there was some doubt about the future of the factory but in the end it survived with the pipeline passing over the Expressway.

The Face to Face Sculpture at the Park Circus Roundabout

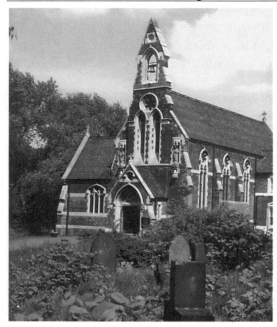

St Joseph's Church

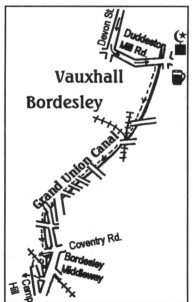

reach another pedestrian crossing. Cross the dual carriageway (Waterlinks Boulevard) noting the 'Locks' roundabout on the left; turn left and follow the pavement round to the right along Lynton Road into Thimble Mill Lane. Walking on the right the road passes over the Aston Relief Arm of the Birmingham and Fazeley canal.

Beside Cheston Road, which you pass on the right, is Hockley Brook in a culvert. Pass Aston Manor Brewery and cross the road to pass St Joseph's R.C. Church and graveyard, where notable Roman Catholic dignitaries are buried. *This graveyard and the Jewish one at Witton are the only ones in the city not maintained by Birmingham City Council.*

Cross Long Acre and continue up Thimble Mill Lane passing a Chinese restaurant, a bank and the Wing Yip Chinese Supermarket *(another indicator of Birmingham's multi-ethnic community)* to reach a roundabout. At the roundabout cross over Nechells Park Road (B4132) on the left and turn right;

Heartlands.

The plan to develop the Eastern side of Birmingham was conceived in 1987 and development began in March 1992. Heartlands covers an area of 2500 acres – bigger than Sutton Park. On the walk we enter Heartlands as we cross the Aston Expressway and leave it at the Coventry Road. Approaching from this direction we are greeted by a modern sculpture 'Face to Face' 1993.

The development has industrial and housing components (Bordesley Village) but the walk only touches on the western part of the development.

pass a bakery on the corner and Pilkington Glass on the left and turn left into Nechells Place.

Follow the road across a railway bridge and round past the gas holders into Cato Street North to pass the Albion Vaults pub and reach and cross the dual carriageway (Saltley Road) at the pedestrian crossing on the left, just before the Sportsman Inn. Past the Sportsman Inn look across to a colourful metal sculpture on a traffic island.

Bus services 14, 56, 90,91 and 92 to Chelmsley Wood and No 8 Inner Circle

Turn left and then immediately right into Devon Street.

The Wing Yip supermarket and restaurant

The Chinese in Birmingham.

The first Chinese restaurant in Birmingham opened in Holloway Head in 1956. Many of the ethnic Chinese, largely from Hong Kong, arrived in the 1960s and 70s. They had no industrial skills but rapidly introduced the local population to Chinese food and opened 'Take-aways'.

Birmingham has become a major centre for the Chinese and there is now a well established community with a Chinese quarter in the city centre.

Approximately 90% are employed in catering and related occupations. The Wing Yip supermarket, which we pass on the walk, is an interesting place to visit.

Wing Yip has donated the 40ft seven-storey stone pagoda which stands in Holloway Circus and marks the city-centre Chinese quarter. It was handmade in East China and shipped over in large sections.

At the highest point in Devon Street, Holy Trinity Church, Camp Hill, for which we are aiming, can be seen ahead on the skyline.

At the end of Devon Street turn left into Duddeston Mill Road. Cross the road to pass Nechells Green Garden Centre on the right and look out for a cul-de-sac on the right beside the River Rea. *The metal gates on the left are opened to allow snow-laden lorries to offload*

Lock on the Grand Union Canal

snow into the river below after a heavy snow-fall. Continuing along the road cross a bridge over the Rea. On the left note a raised pavment under the railway bridge and the wall of Derbyshire blue brick, the green dome of a mosque, and on the sky-line St Saviour's church. Just beyond the pylon turn right down a path to the Birmingham & Warwick Junction section of the Grand Union Canal and walk along the towpath with the canal on your left to pass four locks.

The old industrial scene eventually gives way to modern housing, with a new bridge (102A) named The Village Bridge, opened in 1995, leading across the canal to 'Bordesley Village' with a shopping area, community hall, doctor's surgery and The Sportsman pub. After passing under bridge 98 the junction with the Grand Union Canal, which links Birmingham to London is reached.

Follow the towpath round to the right and then immediately turn right to cross the bridge over the Birmingham & Warwick Junction Canal (i.e. a U-turn). Note the deep grooves in the iron-work of the bridge, caused by the towropes of the horse-drawn canal boats. Walk along the towpath, with the Grand Union Canal on the right, to pass two locks. Beware of a low headroom at bridge 94.

Notice the red doors in the bridge. They were put in during World War II to allow the fire services to obtain water from the canal in an emergency.

Reaching bridge 93 – the number is on the far side – note the damage to the brickwork caused by towropes. Many canal bridges have metal protectors to prevent this. After passing under the bridge reach a third lock and then immediately turn left (i.e. a U-turn) to emerge on the Coventry Road.

Many bus services

Turn *left* and as you reach a railway bridge observe to the right in Upper Trinity Street the old painted sign 'BR(W) BORDESLEY CATTLE STATION'. No signs of cattle today! *Immediately* after passing under the railway bridge turn left again into Bedford Road and follow it round into Trinity Terrace and then uphill, with Trinity Church on the left.

This church has been deconsecrated and currently is being used as a shelter for homeless men (The Trinity Centre).

Turn left and cross the road Old Camp Hill, passing the relatively new Seventh Day Adventist Church on the right, to reach the Brewer and Baker. This is on the site of the original Ship Inn, the headquarters of Prince Rupert during the Civil War.

Many bus services.

The Brewer and Baker at Camp Hill

The Old Ship Inn and Prince Rupert

The inn was probably built as a farmhouse but was converted into a roadside inn in the seventeenth century. It was then surrounded by fields and the garden was a favourite resort of Birmingham tradesmen and artisans. As Thomas Turner, a local historian, described it in a history of the inn published in 1863 "they used to sit and smoke their pipes, with their wives and sweethearts, and talk over the news of the day: indulge in the healthful exercise of a game at bowls or quoits: the children amusing themselves on the green, under the shade of lofty trees, where they were often agreeably disturbed by the sound of the guard's horn, on the arrival and departure of the stage coaches, which called at this house... Here the driver of the fly-wagon to Oxford and London, drawn by six or eight powerful horses, stopped to water them, and take his first foaming tankard, previous to performing three days' tedious journey". Somewhat different from today! – though you can still sit outside the Baker and Brewer on a fine day with your tankard.

But the seventeenth century was a troubled time with six years of Civil War, 1642-1648.

On April 1st 1643 the Old Ship Inn was occupied by Prince Rupert's Royalist advance guard and became his headquarters for several days. Two days later, on Easter Monday, the Royalists began a savage attack on the town that became known as the Battle of Birmingham.

The Ship Inn (from an old engraving).

4

Camp Hill to Cannon Hill Park

2 miles

PASS the Brewer and Baker pub and walk round to the front entrance; turn right to cross the road (Camp Hill) at the pedestrian crossing. To your left you will see the turretted Bordesley Centre, originally the King Edward VI Grammar School and now housing a mosque, conference centre, sports hall and other community services. Turn right and then left into Ravenhurst Street to gain a

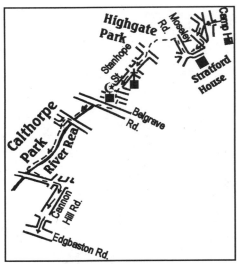

Plaque on the former Lench's Trust almshouses

glimpse of the former Lench's Trust almshouses (1848) on the left corner. Now back-track to the pedestrian crossing – do not cross it but follow the pavement round into Camp Hill/Highgate Middleway and then turn into New Moseley Road on the right. Cross over to enter Stratford Place and view Stratford House (1601).

Stratford House is one of Birmingham's gems, best seen from the green grass opposite.

Cross Moseley Road and turn right; cross over Chandos

Lench's Trust

In 1525 William Lench, who lived in Moor Street placed a number of his properties in the hands of trustees, the rents from these properties to be used for the up-keep of roads and bridges and for various charitable activities. In following years other properties were added and in the early seventeenth century several almshouses were built, including one in Digbeth. Lench's Trust still exists and is the only institution in Birmingham to have survived from medieval times.

Road and walk with park railings on the left *(note the architecture on the opposite side of the road). Aproaching the gate note the view of the City Centre.* Enter Highgate Park at the gate lodge. Immediately turn left and walk along the main drive to the statue of King

Stratford House (from an old engraving)

Highgate Park

Edward VII, erected by public subscription in 1913 in Victoria Square and moved here in 1951. Descend the steps on the right opposite the statue and walk diagonally through the children's playground to a green gate in the fence.

The large red building seen on the right as you descend the steps is the Chamberlain Park Hotel.

Turn left into a new housing development to reach a road opposite numbers 28-50. Turn left again and almost immediately turn left once more and then right through a parking area to leave the development at Darwin Street. Here turn left, cross the road and turn right into Stanhope Street. (The Peacock pub is to the right in Darwin Street.) Cross over Leopold Street, Emily Street and Angelina Street passing St Alban's school on the right and St Albans Church on the left.

Outside the church is a memorial cross to the Pollock brothers who established the first church there in 1865. Their High Church practices resulted in some riotous behaviour from local Low Church opponents!

Ahead the white plastic dome of the Birmingham Central Mosque now comes into view.

Continue along Stanhope Street to reach Conybere Street at a

The Chamberlain Park Hotel

This impressive building was originally the Rowton House Hotel for Poor Men, the first of a number of "poor men's hotels" and the brainchild of two Victorian philanthropists, Lord Rowton and Sir Edward Guiness, who were shocked by the conditions that they had found in many lodging houses. They resolved to create an entirely new class of accommodation and the Rowton House Hotel was built to the design of a London architect, Harry Measures FRIBA. It is an excellent example of Victorian Gothic with outer walls of red Ruabon brick decorated with buff terracotta.

Although the accommodation was from 5/6d to 8/- a week (27½ p. to 40 p.) Rowton House was designed with many of the trappings of the best hotels. The six storey building occupied a fine site overlooking Highgate Park. There were over 800 bedrooms, and although these were spartan they were kept clean and all received air and sunlight during the day. There were reading and writing rooms, a smoking room, a billiards room, a laundry, and a steam heated drying room where residents who had been caught in the rain could have their wet clothes dried free of charge. There was a tailor, a barber and a shoemaker on site.

TARIFF

Subject to slight alteration according to market prices.

BREAKFAST.

BACON. Large Rasher		each 4d.
.. Small ..		2½d.
EGGS. Boiled or Fried		2d.
LIVER & BACON	per portion	5d.
SAUSAGES		each 2½d.
TOMATOES. Cooked	per portion	2½d.
PORRIDGE	.. ..	1½d.

DINNER   (Opening to Closing time).

ROAST BEEF. 2 Vegetables	8d.
.. MUTTON 2 Veg., Mint Sauce	8d.
BEEF STEW. 2 Vegetables.	5d. or 8d.
SPECIAL DAILY DISH from	7d.
MINCE & POTATOES per portion	3½d.
LIVER & BACON	5d.
SAUSAGE (1) & MASH	4d.
SOUP	per basin 2d.

For Fish and other Specials see daily Menu Card.

TEA	per large cup 1d.
COFFEE or COCOA	1½d.
BREAD	per piece 1d. per slice½d.
BREAD or CHARMO (Margarine) 2 slices1½d.	

BUTTER is not spread on slices but is sold in ¼ lb. and 1d. pats.

JAM or MARMALADE	per portion 1d.

TOBACCO and CIGARETTES on Sale.

Women were employed as bed makers but a separate staircase in full view of the main office led to their rooms – to avoid any impropriety!

The foundation stone was laid in 1903 by Princess Helena, the third daughter of Queen Victoria.

It became the Chamberlain Park Hotel in 1993 and now caters for a very different type of customer. As many as possible of the original features have been preserved to retain its original character and it is now a Grade II listed building.

T-junction; cross over the road and take an almost facing tarmac path, and to the left of a building (Magnolia Day Centre). *Here views of South Birmingham appear – note the Joseph Chamberlain Tower at the University of Birmingham.* At the road (Highgate Street) cross over and enter Highgate Close (slightly to the left) following it round to gain Belgrave Middleway (A4540).

Birmingham Central Mosque

This was the first purpose built mosque in Birmingham. Building started in 1968 with the dome being finished in 1982. The minaret is 150 ft high. The mosque can hold up to 2500 people.

Number 8 Inner Circle bus route.

Turn right and walk past the mosque. Cross Gooch Street,

The Chamberlain Park Hotel from Highgate Park

Birmingham Central Mosque

The Inauguration of Calthorpe Park: the Duke of Cambridge planting a tree (as shown in the Illustrated London News, June 13, 1857).

then turn left to cross Belgrave Middleway at pedestrian crossings.

Bus services

Turn right to cross a bridge over the culverted River Rea and

---

Calthorpe Park

A parliamentary act for establishing public parks in Birmingham 'for the purposes of healthful and pleasurable resort' was introduced in 1854 and enabled the Council 'To accept any Gifts, Grants, or Devises of Lands, or to purchase, for a Sum of Money … any Lands, situate in or near Birmingham…' for this purpose.

In 1856 the General Purposes Committee reported to the Council an offer from Lord Calthorpe to let to the Corporation a piece of land in Pershore Road of from 20 to 30 acres for the purposes of public recreation and by way of experiment for one year at a rental of £3 per acre. The offer was accompanied by the following conditions:

1st. That the working classes shall have free admittance at all hours of the day during the six working days.

2nd. That no person shall be admitted to the ground on Sunday.

3rd. That all gambling, indecent language, and disorderly conduct be strictly prohibited.

4th. That no wine, malt liquor or spirituous liquor be sold or consumed on the ground.

5th. That no smoking be allowed.

6th. That no horses and carriages be permitted to enter the grounds, except chairs on wheels with invalids and children.

7th. That no dogs be permitted to enter.

8th. That no games be allowed except cricket, rounders, trap ball, battledore, quoits, gymnastics and archery.

9th. That bathing be prohibited.

10th. That Sunday and day-school children be admitted on the days of their anniversary.

11th. That a proper number of police officers be in attendance, strictly to enforce the above regulations.

12th That the fences be preserved from injury.

These conditions were considerably modified at the request of the Council and the offer was ultimately accepted.

immediately turn left to follow a path parallel with the river. Reaching Balsall Heath Road turn right, cross the road and turn left into Alexandra Road, where, on the left, there is a complex of accommodation for people of Chinese origin (Connaught Gardens).

Do not follow the road as it bends round the corner to become Speedwell Road, but continue the line of Alexandra Road to enter Calthorpe Park. Walk through the park with the metal fence on the left, following the line of the River Rea. Turn left to cross the bridge over the river and enter a children's playground just before reaching Edward Road.

Cross the playground and then veer right at the play centre to enter Edward Road; turn left and follow the road to view the Victorian urinal on the right side of Court Road. Cross over Edward Road and turn back towards the river, but then turn left immediately into Cannon Hill Road. Continue, crossing Willows Crescent, and passing the Warwickshire County Cricket ground on the right to reach Edgbaston Road. Cannon Hill Park, the next stage of our walk is across on the other side of the road.

Bus service 1

Warwickshire County Cricket Ground

Warwickshire County Cricket Club was formed in 1882 by the efforts of William Ansell. Lord Calthorpe offered the club a piece of rough grazing land in Edgbaston and the present ground was opened in 1886, the first match being played in June of that year against the MCC with 3000 watching. Ansell worked tirelessly to obtain recognition for Warwickshire as a first class county club, rather than a second class one and succeeded in 1894. The first test match was played there in 1902, though this was not a very promising start – the weather proved disastrous and the event made a loss of £2,000.

5

Cannon Hill Park to Bournville

3½ miles

ENTER Cannon Hill Park through the main gates. Once in the park turn right, crossing the cycle track. Follow this path, signed Nature Centre and MAC (for Midlands Arts Centre), round to the right, passing a pool on the right. Turn right, skirting the pool, and continue straight ahead to reach the model of the Elan Valley Waterworks – the main source of water for the City of Birmingham. Carry on along this path, with a wooded area to the right and a low wall on the left, pausing to read the plaque

---

Cannon Hill Park

The land for this park was given to Birmingham in 1872 by Miss Louisa Ann Ryland. She declined to have her name associated with the park and there was no opening ceremony. She was active in planning the lay-out of the park which has two boating lakes, beautiful trees and shrubs and is arguably the most attractive of the city's parks.

It is thought that part of the royalist army camped on this site before the battle of Naseby in 1645.

In the park is the Boer War Memorial and between the park and the Nature Centre is the Boy Scout memorial commemorating those who gave their lives in both World Wars.

In 1911 the Golden Lion Inn, a fifteenth century half-timbered building, was moved to the park from Digbeth It is thought that originally it may have been a clergy house and school of the guild of St John Deritend.

A model of the Elan valley waterworks was constructed to commemorate the completion of the final stages of the development and as a tribute to the pioneers of the scheme, which was commenced in 1892, inaugurated in 1904 and completed in 1952. The model was completed in 1961: sadly at the time of writing it is in less good shape than the scheme which it commemorates.

MAC (Midlands Arts Centre)

Situated in Cannon Hill Park MAC was opened as a centre for young people in 1964 on the site of a former bathing pool and later a zoo. Its aim was to 'promote innovative, creative arts activities in ways which would help to establish them as an important part of people's lives'.

The centre has auditoria, exhibition spaces, studios, workshop and rehearsal areas and a number of informal spaces for performances. In addition it has a bar, a café, and a bookshop.

It continues to be a centre attracting people of all ages and abilities from the multi-ethnic community, fostering active participation in practical activities.

The 130 classes held each week include pottery, painting, textiles, dance, drama, music, Yoga and Tai Chi. In addition there are excellent cinema programmes and theatrical productions.

providing information about the extent of the Elan Valley and the Waterworks.

Continuing to the right, join the main path round a boating lake. *(Note the Boer War memorial on the opposite side of the lake)*. Walk with the water on the left and a wooded area to the right. At the end of this lake, MAC is on the right – *toilets, restaurant, bookshop, cinema, theatre, exhibitions and information are all gathered here.*

From MAC walk between the two lakes and turn right to walk

'Erratic' in Cannon Hill Park

The confluence of the Bourn Brook with the Rea

with the water on the right. You will pass a large boulder in the grass on the left – this is an *erratic*, deposited here during the last ice age and having been brought down by a glacier from the Arenig Mountains in North Wales. There are several of these in and around Birmingham – we shall meet another one later in the walk. Further to the left, across the grass, note the Golden Lion, a fifteenth century inn, originally situated in Deritend.

Holders Wood

The River Rea

Historically this river, on which Birmingham is built, has been very important. It formed the boundary between the parishes of Aston and Birmingham in the north, and Warwickshire and Worcestershire in the south.

In the middle ages drovers used to get livestock across at the ford in Deritend. Its source is in the Waseley Hills (Grid Reference 975872) and it flows through South Birmingham, Deritend and Aston to enter the River Tame about three-quarters of a mile to the east of this walk.

Over the centuries a lot of changes have taken place to and around the River Rea. There were many water mills along its bank e.g. Pebble Mill. In 1875 the river was 'culverted' under Lawley Street marshalling yards and between 1890 and 1904 the whole Rea was channelled in redbrick, apart from the length at Cannon Hill Park where stone was used. Two loops of the river were filled in – at the county cricket ground and at Calthorpe Park. To cope with flooding the channel had to be deepened.

Today much of the channelling has been removed. We have the Rea Valley cycle track and the river can be walked for much of its length as we see on the southern part of this walk

The River Rea

At the end of the lake turn right and cross over the bridge; continue straight on to a second bridge (over the River Rea). Do not cross it, but instead turn left and go down steps on the right to the river. Turn left to walk with the river on the right. Soon the Bourn Brook will be seen on the right cascading down to join the Rea. Soon follow the incline up to the bridge, then turn left and immediately right . Almost at once turn left onto a grass track between parallel low wooden fencing.

At the end of the railings turn right and continue on the main track, shortly crossing a concrete footbridge. After about 50 yards, at a Y-junction of paths, go left to reach, after about 75 yards, a cross-paths beside a seat. (*When the leaves are off the trees, Chamberlain Tower at Birmingham University and the B.B.C. building at Pebble Mill can be seen to the* right.) Now go left along a well trodden path to walk with a wire fence and allotments on the left. Continue to a T-junction at a tarmac path, turn left, passing through traffic-calming barriers. At the next T-junction, cross diagonally to take a track opposite, which leads past a British Gas building into Holder's Wood.

Carry on along the main path through the centre of the wood, parallel with the road.

Following paths through a wood can sometimes be rather confusing. However, if you are uncertain at any point remember that the route is forward, through the wood, to emerge into a field at the far end.

A small pond soon appears on the right. Cross a bridge, immediately go left at a Y-junction of paths and in about 40 yards cross another bridge. After about 50 yards, at another Y-junction (with a green shed and a pool to the right), go left and walk with houses over to the left for about 250 yards, ignoring paths off, to emerge into a field. Follow the path as it bends to the right across the field and then passes through a gap in a hedge. Keep on the main path to reach a tarmac path; cross it and follow the path facing – there is a large tree on the right – to a path T-junction.

Here turn left; just before gaining a driveway leading to the road at the Highbury Inn turn right onto another path and follow it to gain Moor Green Lane at its junction with Dogpool Lane.

The Cadbury Works

What is now Cadbury Schweppes moved from premises in Bridge Street near the City Centre in 1879 to a fourteen acre site in the south of the city – what might now be called a green field site – with 230 employees involved in the production of cocoa and chocolate.

The proximity of the canal system, which facilitated transport, was a factor in the choice of site and then the transport situation was further improved with the opening of Bournville railway station.

The name of the firm became Cadbury Brothers Ltd. in 1899. In addition to setting up the Bournville Village Trust in 1900 (see below) Cadburys was involved in many social improvements for its workers –

for example it was the first firm in the city to introduce half day closing on a Saturday; a bath house for girl employees was built 1902-1904; the Rowheath playing fields were developed 1919-1924.

Originally involved in the production of cocoa, sweet production was added in 1880; Dairy Milk Chocolate was added in 1904, Milk Tray in 1915 and Roses in 1983. The works were enlarged at the beginning of the century and re-built 1923-1939. The merger with Schweppes took place in 1969.

More recently a Visitor Centre, Cadbury World, showing the production of chocolate from the cocoa bean in South America to the final product has opened.

Bus services 69/69A .

Turn right and walk up to bollards adjacent to a bridge over the River Rea. Cross the road and take the tarmac Rea Valley foot and cycle way to the left of the bridge. The river is now no longer culverted and is flowing naturally. Reaching the first footbridge cross this and now walk with the river on your left to reach Cartland Road.

Bus service 35.

Cross the road and continue along the Rea Valley route through Hazelwell Recreation Ground. After passing an imaginative children's play area (The Dragon's Lair) reach a bridge on the right. Cross it and Hunt's Road to enter Hazelwell Lane opposite.

Bournville Village

In 1895 George Cadbury bought land near to the Bournville factory to build a model village with the object of '...alleviating the evils which arise from the insanitary and insufficient housing accommodation supplied to large numbers of the working classes, and of securing to workers in factories some of the advantages of outdoor village life ...'

Building of semi-detached houses began towards the end of the century and in 1900 George Cadbury set up the Bournville Village Trust which is independent from the factory. 313 dwellings were built in 330 acres of land with the aim of providing high quality housing for a socially mixed community. Houses were provided with gardens of an adequate size for growing produce, and gardening skills were encouraged. Rather than spend money on drink, tenants would spend their leisure hours in more productive and healthy activities.

The tenants were not restricted to Cadbury employees and their families but priority was given to families with insufficient means to provide for themselves. This was in contrast to Port Sunlight where housing was only available for Lever employees. The estate has expanded during the century and by 1991 had 1000 acres of land with 8000 dwellings.

The village is centred around The Green in the middle of which is a Rest House, funded by Cadbury employees world-wide to commemorate the Silver Wedding of George and Elizabeth Cadbury in 1913. Adjacent to The Green is Bournville Junior school with its Carillon – recently refurbished.

Walk up Hazelwell Lane to the Pershore Road at Stirchley.

🚌 *Several bus services to City Centre.*

At this point buildings opposite result in the road functioning as a dual carriageway. To get to the other side, turn right and walk to a pedestrian crossing; cross the road to the Three Horseshoes pub, turn left along the Pershore Road (here Hazelwell Street), cross Umberslade Road and pass a supermarket to reach the Friends Meeting House and the now closed Public Baths on the corner of Bournville Lane. Turn right

Minworth Greaves (left) and Selly Manor (right)

Selly Manor and Minworth Greaves

Selly Manor was moved from its original site in Bournbrook by George Cadbury at the beginning of this century, being transported brick by brick. It was a tithing house and there are records of its existence going back to 1327. It was opened to the public in 1917 and houses the Laurence Cadbury collection of furniture dating from around 1500 to 1750.

Minworth Greaves is an even older house dating back to 1250. Sadly only the cruck beamed great hall had survived when George Cadbury rescued it from its original site in Curdworth. It was re-built beside Selly Manor by Laurence Cadbury in 1932.

and walk up the road, noting the 'Bournville Market, 1900' plaque at the corner of Bond Street and passing under the railway and canal bridge at Bournville station.

Bus service 35.

Cross City line.

Shortly, the first of a series of notices appears highlighting places and events in the development of what is now Cadbury Schweppes, whose territory we are about to enter.

There is a permissive pathway through to Cadbury World and Bournville Village Green. Should it be closed, continue along Bournville Lane to a crossroads and turn right along Linden Road to reach the Village Green where the route taking the permissive path joins and this section of the walk ends.

To use the permissive path, turn right into Main Street South, cross the road and follow the pavement on the left and di-

The Bournville Carillon

rections for Cadbury World. Turn the corner left into Lodge Street West (Bird Cage Walk) and then cross the road at the pedestrian crossing to the pavement on the right (*strong smell of chocolate here at times*). Turn right through traffic barriers (still Bird Cage Walk and following the Cadbury World signs), cross the Bourn and continue round the corner to the end of the factory buildings. Cross the road at the pedestrian crossing and turn right – sign-posted Bournville Village and Selly Manor. On reaching Sycamore Road in Bournville Village the permissive path ends.

Although only developed towards the end of the last century, when Richard and George Cadbury moved the chocolate factory to a then green-belt site, Bournville, with its centre at The Green, is worth taking time to explore. On the right is Selly Manor, an original timber-framed building moved from its original site in Bournbrook and now housing a museum. Behind it is Minworth Greaves, an even earlier building moved from Curdworth. Ahead is The Green, with a rest house reputed to have been built with halfpennies donated by factory workers to celebrate the Silver Wedding anniversary of George Cadbury and his wife in 1913. Around The Green and nearby are more modern buildings of architectural interest and the schools and some of the housing of this model village are seen as the walk proceeds. The Green is at its best in spring when the daffodils are in bloom. There is a coffee lounge in the block of shops on the left, facing The Green and there is a restaurant and shop at the entrance to Cadbury World.

Cross Sycamore Road and turn left to cross The Green to the rest house. Circle it to reach Linden Road, on the opposite side of which can be seen Bournville Junior and Infant Schools. Note the fine clock which also has a carillon of bells that you might be fortunate enough to hear. To the left of the clock is the entrance into Bournville Park and the starting point for the next section of our walk.

Bus Outer Circle route 11A/11C.

6

Bournville to Cofton Park

5½ miles

F ROM Linden Road, opposite St Francis' church and the main entrance to Cadbury World, turn into Bournville Park. Take the first path on the left and walk diagonally to cross a bridge over the Bourn.

The Bourn is not to be confused with the Bourn Brook which flows further north; the Bourn is the continuation of Griffins Brook, as it flows through Bournville – its name is said to have been changed at the request of Cadburys.

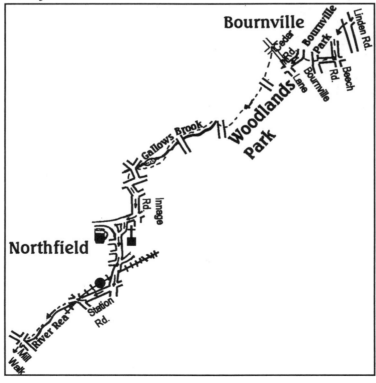

Continue straight ahead into Beech Road as far as house number 13 on the right and immediately turn right into a walkway. Continue across Selly Oak Road to follow the walkway between numbers 56 and 60; keep to the line of the walkway across the grass into Cedar Road and turn left to walk to a crossroads. Here turn right along Bournville Lane

Cross the road and immediately after number 201 turn left along another walkway. When the tarmac path swings right into Berberry Close continue forward along an unsurfaced path (wire fence on the left) to reach Woodlands Park. Follow the tarmac path through the park with the brook on the left, to Woodlands Park Road

35 bus route.

Cross the road and continue along a further tarmac walkway. Cross two bridges, turn left and follow the walkway through to Hole Lane. Cross the road, turn right and immediately take the walkway on the left. At the mini-roundabout turn left and, passing a pool, cross a footbridge.

Across the bridge turn right beside the pool, noting another large stone beside the pool. Join the flagged Garland Way and turn right, now with a stream on your right. At a path crossing turn right and again cross to a bridge with a metal rail; turn sharp left to follow a track through a wooded area. Climb up four steps on the left just before a brick bridge, immediately cross a narrow path and swing right across a grassed area to St Laurence Road at St Joseph's Avenue. Cross St Laurence Road to enter Victoria Common through a metal gate.

Modern Northfield is ahead and a diversion may be made here to visit the Grosvenor Shopping Centre, and the Bristol Road, where there are a number of pubs, cafés, toilets and buses.

Bus services 18, 61, 62, 63.

To reach Northfield, follow the tarmac path, passing a children's play area. At a T-junction turn right; continue past tennis courts skirting a playing field and turn right at the second set of tennis courts to reach the back of the shopping centre. Then retrace your steps to return to the main walk.

On entering Victoria Common, follow the fence on the left, across grass, round a corner to leave the Common by a metal gate. In Heath Road, cross over the road and walk up Dinmore Avenue to Innage Road. Turn right to gain Bunbury Road. Again turn right and cross Bunbury road at a pedestrian crossing. Turn right and continue to Rectory Road. Turn left and follow the road round to the right.

Opposite the entrance to St Laurence church a brief diversion may be made to the right to look at the old village pound and another erratic stone (The Great Stone, from which the name of the nearby pub is derived) deposited at the end of the last ice age. Return to the

Northfield Church

gate of the church and follow the road round to the right, noting the old houses. Continue down the hill and under the railway bridge and turn right into Station Road.

Bus services 35, 44.

Northfield station – Cross-city line on the right.

When you reach a T-junction pass under another railway bridge. Using the traffic lights, *carefully* cross over Quarry Lane and Mill Lane. Immediately at the traffic lights enter a wooded walkway on the left; follow it past the site of the old Northfield Mill, up steps and continue forward with the River Rea on the left and Mill Lane on the right until you reach a ford on the left at The Mill Walk.

The 'Erratic' in the Northfield Village Pound

Continue ahead through Kalamazoo (the footpath here is a public Right of Way) with the River Rea on the left. Continue between the metal fencing taking the line of the main path through a car park (Park Walk) and Daffodil Park to reach Tessall Lane.

Turn left and cross the road to gain a footbridge beside metal gates and continue to the right to reach Longbridge Lane adjacent to Longbridge station.

🚂 *Cross-city line.*
🚌 *Bus services 44/85/86.*

At the T-junction carefully cross Longbridge Lane (dual carriageway) turn left and cross the *old* bridge over the railway (*not the mod-*

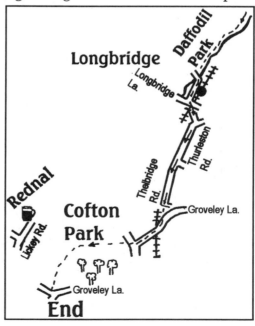

59

Kalamzoo

Kalamazoo was established in Edmund St in Birmingham in 1896 with a capital of £12,500 as Morland and Impey.

In 1904 the firm became interested in advertisements for Twin Lock and Kalamazoo loose-leaf systems, which were not available in England. After a visit to America the firm was sufficiently impressed by the Kalamazoo system to purchase £400 of goods which arrived in England in spring of 1905 and subsequently purchased the sales rights for world wide distribution outside America from the Kalamazoo Binder Co. of Michigan U.S.A. for £4000.

The company moved to its present site in the nineteen twenties and in the seventies there was extensive new building. Today the company is involved in working on computer solutions for the motor industry.

ern one which is straight ahead but the earlier one to the right). On the *right* take a flagged path between Greenlands Social Club and a filling station to reach Falfield Grove. Follow this road to a T-junction and turn right into Thurlestone Road and then, after about 350 yards, right into Thelbridge Road, which leads into Fountain Close with its more modern housing.

At number 37 turn right into a paved walkway. Very shortly.

The Rover Works at Longbridge

The works were established in 1905 by Herbert (later Lord) Austin) and the first car was produced in 1905. Since then the firm has changed its name and the type of car produced. Recently owned by the German car manufacturing firm BMW the Rover Works were saved from closure in 2000 by their purchase by the Phoenix Consortium.

One of the earliest cars produced was the Baby Austin (Austin Seven) in 1922 (retailing at around £168) and in 1931 it was the first car to reach a speed of 100 m.p.h. In 1952 the firm merged with its great rival the Morris motor company in Oxford to form the British Motoring Corporation and in 1959 the world famous mini, designed by the late Sir Alec Issigonis was launched.

The firm expanded and became British Leyland. In 1980 the Mini Metro was introduced with robots doing most of the work.

Austin was one of the first firms to introduce a night shift.

Lickey Hills

In 1919 the Cadbury family gave the 520 acres of the Lickey Hills to the City of Birmingham (although 90 per cent of the land is in Worcestershire). The Lickeys are now a Country Park managed by the Leisure and Community Services Dept of Birmingham City Council. The description 'Birmingham's lung' has been used! A popular family outing in the early part of the twentieth century was a tram ride to the Lickeys.

The hills are an H-shaped sandstone outcrop, covered with conifers, birches and bracken. Beacon Hill is the highest point at 965 ft and from here there are excellent and extensive views for those wishing to extend the walk.

at a path Y-junction turn left and follow the now unpaved path past Clark's Body Repair Centre on the right to a T-junction (Groveley Lane); cross the road and turn right. *(The road is crossed for reasons of safety; the observant will notice that we also cross the Birmingham boundary for a short distance. Ahead can be seen the Lickey Hills.)*

Pass the Rover distribution centre, cross the railway line, then pass the Rover works to reach another T-junction (Groveley Lane/Lowhill Lane).

The two groups of conifers in Cofton Park

Bus Services 47/145

Cross the road *very carefully* and enter Cofton Park ahead. Continue straight ahead, passing a house (Lowhill Farm) on the right; walk uphill between the two groups of nine conifers ahead (*these may be somewhat obscured when trees are in leaf*); then continue diagonally to the left (*ten o'clock* using clock configuration).

A row of houses soon comes into view ahead – aim to the rightmost of these. Climb up a bank and continue forward to cross a tarmac path; continue diagonally left and the end of the walk is in sight. Walk to the main road – still Groveley Lane – and the Birmingham/Worcestershire Boundary at Ten Ashes Lane.

This is where the walk finishes but to regain public transport etc. retrace your steps to the tarmac path, turn left along it and follow it to the end in Rednal where you will find a pub, the Old Hare and Hounds, and refreshments.

Cross the road at the pedestrian crossing and turn right to reach the number 62 bus stop.

The 62 bus goes down the Bristol Road through Northfield and Selly Oak to the City Centre.

If you wish to transfer to the train (Cross-City Line) this is most conveniently done at Selly Oak where the station is close to the bus route.

The end of the walk at the city boundary

WALKS AROUND THE MALVERNS

by Roy Woodcock

The Malvern Hills and their surroundings provide magnificent opportunities for rambling, and in this book of twenty walks Roy Woodcock explores many of their superb features. The walks cover the entire range of hills and the neighbouring commons, together with some of the delightful countryside nearby. Distances range from two miles to eight miles, plus a leg stretcher of between ten and sixteen miles (depending on the starting point) that takes in the full length of the ridge and ascends all the Malvern peaks.

ISBN 1 869922 32 8. £5.95. 112 pages. 32 illustrations. 20 maps.

WATERSIDE WALKS IN THE MIDLANDS

by Birmingham Ramblers: edited by Peter Groves

Twenty-two walks featuring brooks, streams, pools, rivers and canals. Some can be found a short distance from the centre of Britain's second city; others will take the reader further afield in the West Midlands and into the attractive counties of Warwickshire, Worcestershire, Shropshire, Staffordshire and Derbyshire.

ISBN 1 869922 09 3. £4.95. 112 pages. 28 photographs. 22 maps.

MORE WATERSIDE WALKS IN THE MIDLANDS

by Birmingham Ramblers: edited by Peter Groves

A second collection of walks featuring brooks, streams, rivers, canals and pools. Most are circular, the three exceptions having ample public transport to the start and at the finish. Distances range from 4½ miles to14 miles.

ISBN 1 869922 31 X. £5.95 112 pages. 21 photographs. 18 maps.

WALKS TO WET YOUR WHISTLE

by Roger Seedhouse

Eighteen walks covering some of the most beautiful countryside in Shropshire and along its Staffordshire borders, each providing an opportunity to visit a pub in which the walker will feel welcome and comfortable. The main walks range in distance between 7 and 11½ miles but each has a shorter alternative of between 2¾ and 5¼ miles.

ISBN 1 869922 34 4. £6.95. 112 pages. 17 photos. 18 maps.

MORE WALKS TO WET YOUR WHISTLE

by Roger Seedhouse

Following the author's highly successful first book he now presents a second collection of walks with a pub in Shropshire and along its Staffordshire borders.

ISBN 1 869922 36 0. £6.95. 112 pages. 24 photos. 18 maps.

AND THE ROAD BELOW

by John Westley

The entrancing account of the first complete walk around the coastline of the British Isles, a distance of 9,469 miles, that earned for the author a place in the Guinness Book of Records. Undertaken in aid of multiple sclerosis this book shows how a relatively inexperienced walker could, with courage and an over-riding determination to succeed, overcome what seemed at times to be near-insurmountable problems. The author has donated half his royalties from the sale of this book to the Multiple Sclerosis Society and this sum will be matched by an equal contribution from the publishers.

ISBN 1 869922 25 5. £8.95. 208 pages. 11 photos.

Prices applicable July 2000 and may be subject to change.

Available from booksellers or direct from Meridian Books. Please send remittance, adding for postage & packing, £1.00 for one book, £2.00 for two or more books, to:

Meridian Books
40 Hadzor Road, Oldbury, West Midlands B68 9LA

Please send for our complete catalogue.